Climbing Out of the Great Depression

The New Deal

Sean Price

Chicago, Illinois

RAINTREE

TO ORDER:

☎ Phone Customer Service **888-454-2279**

💻 Visit **www.heinemannraintree.com** to browse our catalog and order online.

©2009 Raintree
a division of Pearson Education Limited
Chicago, Illinois

Editorial: Adam Miller
Design: Ryan Frieson, Kimberly R. Miracle, and Betsy Wernert
Photo Research: Tracy Cummins
Production: Victoria Fitzgerald

Originated by DOT Gradations Ltd
Printed and bound by Leo Paper Group

ISBN-13: 978-1-4109-3112-2 (hc)
ISBN-10: 1-4109-3112-9 (hc)
ISBN-13: 978-1-4109-3121-4 (pb)
ISBN-10: 1-4109-3121-8 (pb)

13 12 11 10 09
10 9 8 7 6 5 4 3 2 1

Library of Congress Cataloging-in-Publication Data
Price, Sean.
   Climbing out of the Great Depression : the New Deal / Sean Price.
      p. cm. -- (American history through primary sources)
   Includes bibliographical references and index.
ISBN 978-1-4109-3112-2 (hc : alk. paper) -- ISBN 978-1-4109-3121-4 (pb : alk. paper) 1. United States--History--1933-1945--Sources--Juvenile literature. 2. United States--History--1919-1933--Sources--Juvenile literature. 3. New Deal, 1933-1939--Sources--Juvenile literature. 4. Roosevelt, Franklin D. (Franklin Delano), 1882-1945--Sources--Juvenile literature. 5. Depressions--1929--United States--Sources--Juvenile literature. 6. United States--Economic conditions--1918-1945--Sources--Juvenile literature. I. Title.
   E806.P77 2008
   973.917--dc22

                    2008011424

Acknowledgments
The author and publisher are grateful to the following for permission to reproduced copyright material: ©AP Photo **p. 11**; ©Corbis **pp. 15, 19, 20, 26**; ©Corbis **6, 9-T, 12, 13, 22–23, 25** (Bettmann), **14** (David J. & Janice L. Frent Collection); ©Franklin D. Roosevelt Presidential Library **pp. 21-B, 27**; ©Getty Images **pp. 9-B** (MPI), **10** (FPG); ©Getty Images/Time Life Pictures **pp. 24** (Herbert Gehr), **29** (Al Freni); ©The Granger Collection p. 5; ©Library of Congress Prints and Photographs Division **pp. 4, 7-B, 8, 16, 17-L, 17-R, 18, 21-T, 28**; ©National Archives **p. 7-T.**

Cover image of President Franklin D. Roosevelt meeting with farmers (near Warm Springs, Georgia, October 23, 1932), used with permission of ©Getty Images/FPG

The publishers would like to thank Nancy Harris for her assistance in the preparation of this book.

Contents

Some words are printed in bold, **like this**. You can find out what they mean on page 30. You can also look in the box at the bottom of the page where they first appear.

Crash!

The United States enjoyed good times in the 1920s. Most Americans had jobs. They could buy things like homes and cars.

Some people tried to get rich by buying shares of **stock**. Owning a share of stock makes a person part-owner of a company. If the company does well, the stock price goes up. If it does poorly, the stock price goes down. People buy and sell shares of stock on the **stock market**.

The stock market crash was was big news. It led to the Great Depression.

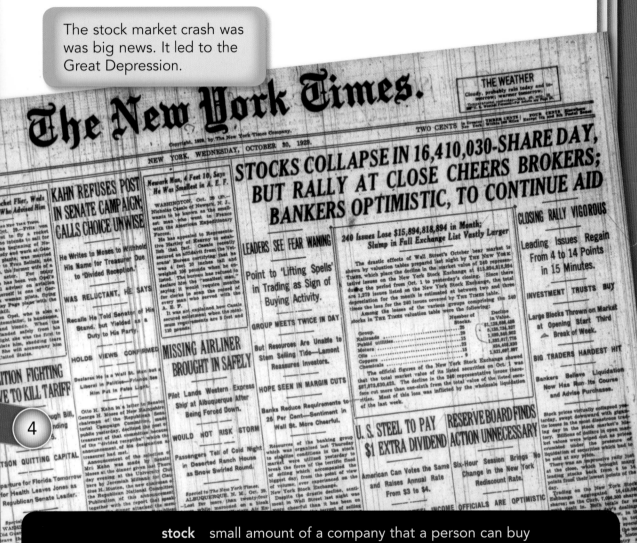

| stock | small amount of a company that a person can buy |
| stock market | place to sell stocks |

Many people lost all of their money. They had to sell their belongings just to survive.

In October 1929, stock prices suddenly fell very fast. The stock market "crashed." This hurt the rest of the U.S. banks who had bought stocks. When stock prices fell, the banks lost all their money. Those banks had to close. People could not get their money out of the bank. Neither could companies. Without money, companies could not hire people.

By 1933, one out of four Americans had no work. They lost their cars and homes. This terrible time was called the **Great Depression**.

Great Depression   time in the 1930s when many people were out of work

Hoovervilles

Herbert Hoover was the **president** of the United States. He led the country. He tried to end the **Great Depression**. But nothing he did worked. Instead, people blamed Hoover for their problems.

The Great Depression made many people poor. They lost their jobs. Then they lost their homes. Some had to live in shacks. Many people built their shacks close together in **Hoovervilles**. These areas were named after the president.

This Hooverville was in New York City. Life was tough under these conditions.

president leader of the United States
Hooverville area where poor people built shacks during the Great Depression

People had little money for food. They needed to ask for free food. Free food was passed out at **bread lines**. Dorothea Lange was a photographer. She took pictures of people standing in bread lines. She showed that times were hard.

People leaving the Dust Bowl were called "Okies." That is because many were from Oklahoma.

These people are waiting in a bread line for free food.

The Dust Bowl

In the 1930s, dust storms swept the country. Most storms happened between the states of Texas and North Dakota. This included the states of Oklahoma, New Mexico, Colorado, Kanasas, Nebraska, Wyoming, and South Dakota. People called this area the **"Dust Bowl."** Many farmers had to leave Dust Bowl states. They could not farm anymore. Lange took pictures of these poor farmers as well.

bread line   place where free food was passed out
Dust Bowl   area in the middle U.S. where dust storms forced people to leave

Happy Days Are Here Again!

The United States elected a new **president** (leader) in 1932. His name was Franklin Roosevelt. Roosevelt helped people feel better. He told them to no longer be afraid, because he planned to make big changes.

Roosevelt moved quickly. His first 100 days in office were very busy. Roosevelt got many new **laws** (rules) approved. These laws created new jobs. The laws Roosevelt passed became known as the "New Deal."

Roosevelt sometimes had a musical band with him. The band would play the same song. The song was called "Happy Days Are Here Again." One verse goes:

"Happy days are here again

The skies above are clear again

So let's sing a song of cheer again

Happy days are here again."

The song, "Happy Days Are Here Again," was very popular.

law   rule

Fireside Chats

There was no television in the 1930s. Instead, people listened to radio. Roosevelt spoke on the radio often. He called his talks "**Fireside Chats**." Roosevelt was a good speaker. His Fireside Chats made people feel better.

Roosevelt used radio speeches to tell Americans what he planned to do.

Fireside Chat radio speech by President Franklin D. Roosevelt

9

A popular president

President Roosevelt received more mail than any president before. His wife, Eleanor, received more mail than any **First Lady** (wife of the president). They received boxes full of mail each day. People wrote because they liked the Roosevelts. "In the strangest way I feel that I know you," one woman wrote to Eleanor. Others felt that way as well.

Many letters came from people who were poor. They asked the Roosevelts for help. They needed money and food. The Roosevelts could not help people directly. But President Roosevelt made new **laws** (rules) that did help people.

President Roosevelt meets with some farmers in Georgia.

First Lady   wife of the president

Eleanor Roosevelt meets with a group of young women. She is wearing a hat and is sitting in the center of the picture.

President Roosevelt met with people who faced hard times. Farmers could not sell crops. Roosevelt listened to them. He passed laws that helped farmers. Eleanor also listened to people. She tried to create programs that gave people jobs. In the photo above, she met with a group of young women. They had no jobs. But they were learning how to find work.

11

Alphabet Soup

The New Deal caused the U.S. **government** to grow. The government is a group of people that run the country. Many new government **agencies** were created. An agency is a part of the government. Each agency has a job. One agency was the Federal Emergency Relief Administration (**FERA**). Its job was to help the poorest people. It gave them food and shelter.

Businesses hung the NRA sign. This showed that they followed the NRA's new rules.

Another agency was the National Recovery Administration (**NRA**). It led one of the biggest New Deal programs. The NRA's job was to help businesses. They helped them create jobs. The NRA symbol was a blue eagle. Companies that followed NRA rules put a blue eagle in their windows.

People called New Deal agencies by their initials. The Federal Emergency Relief Administration was called FERA. The National Recovery Administration was called the NRA. There were many more agencies. All their initials confused people. They called the New Deal "alphabet soup."

The NRA's blue eagle became a very common sight.

NRA National Recovery Administration

CCC

The **Great Depression** was hard on young people. Young men could not find jobs.

President Roosevelt started the Civilian Conservation Corps (**CCC**). Its job was spelled out in its name. A **civilian** is someone who is not in the army or navy. **Conservation** means saving or helping nature. And a **corps** is a group. So the CCC was a group of young men. They did a lot to help nature. They planted trees. Many cleared paths for telephone lines. They made hiking trails and parks.

The CCC gave young men jobs when jobs were hard to find.

CCC Civilian Conservation Corps
civilian someone who is not in the army or navy
conservation saving or helping nature
corps group

Young men were proud to be part of the CCC.

The CCC also had education classes. Many young men could not read or write. The CCC taught them. A lot of young men had never left home before. The CCC showed them places they might never have visited.

The CCC's work can still be seen. They made campgrounds for many state parks. The group built roads and saved forests. The CCC's work allows Americans to visit natural places today.

15

WPA

The Works Progress Administration (**WPA**) was the biggest New Deal **agency**. Its role was to help those who had lost jobs because of the **Great Depression**. The WPA created jobs. It created them in many different areas of life.

Some WPA workers built roads and schools. Others taught acting or wrote books. Still others fed hungry children. Most WPA jobs involved building things. Many schools used today were built by the WPA. So are many government buildings.

The WPA helped poor people in many different ways. They even built homes for the poor.

LOW RENT WOODHILL HOMES

2567 WOODHILL ROAD

CLEVELAND METROPOLITAN HOUSING AUTHORITY

Artists also worked for the WPA. Some artists made **murals**. A mural is a large painting on a wall. WPA artists created posters, as well. The posters advertised government programs. WPA posters could be seen all over the country.

One of the most unusual WPA jobs was in the state of Kentucky. People there lived far apart. They had no libraries. So women rode on horseback to deliver books. They delivered to homes. They also delivered books to one-room schoolhouses.

SEE AMERICA
WELCOME TO MONTANA
U.S. TRAVEL BUREAU

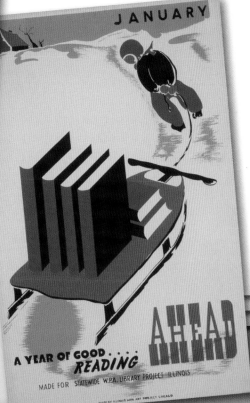

JANUARY

A YEAR OF GOOD... READING
AHEAD
MADE FOR STATEWIDE W.P.A. LIBRARY PROJECT ILLINOIS

Artists had a hard time finding jobs during the Great Depression. Many made posters for the WPA. Those posters told people about the New Deal Programs.

mural large painting on a wall

NYA

The National Youth Administration (**NYA**) helped young people. The NYA was different from the **CCC** (Civilian Conservation Corps). It helped women as well as men. Also, the NYA focused on helping people get through school. It helped students in high school and college.

Many NYA jobs were located at schools. The schools put students to work in part-time jobs. Students did things to help run the school. They might put books back on library shelves. They might help keep the school clean.

The NYA did not only give young people jobs. It gave them things to do in their spare time.

Helen Farmer held an NYA job in the city of Los Angeles. She did a lot of typing for her high school. "It got necessary work done," she said. "It gave teenagers a chance to work for pay." Helen used her money to buy clothes and shoes. Sometimes she used it to go to the movies or buy a candy bar. This helped Helen's mother. She did not have to give Helen money.

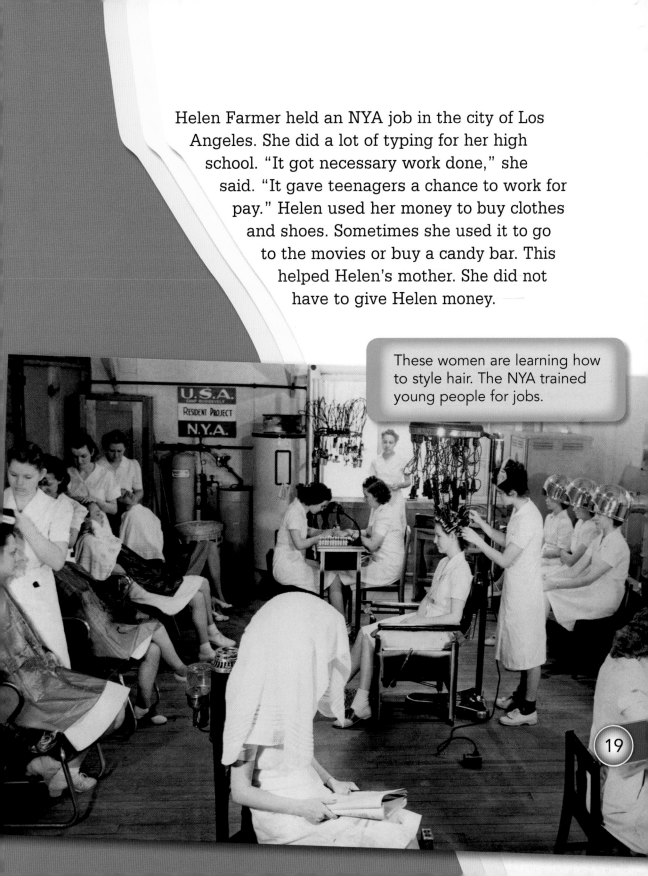

These women are learning how to style hair. The NYA trained young people for jobs.

19

TVA

The Tennessee River flooded a lot. It flooded farms and cities. The Tennessee Valley Authority (**TVA**) built **dams**. Dams are giant walls that hold back water. They are used to control flooding on rivers. Building these dams gave people jobs.

The dams do more than control flooding. Water can pour through one small part of a dam. This water moves fast. It can spin machines. This can create electric power.

The TVA gave many people jobs. It took a lot of people to build a dam!

TVA Tennessee Valley Authority
dam giant wall that holds back water

Dams built by the TVA controlled flooding.

The dams also created electric power. The farm in this picture did not have electric power before.

Many people in Tennessee did not have electric power before. The TVA made it possible for them to get it. People had electric lights and radios for the first time.

The TVA's power also created jobs. Businesses could get electric power. They could set up **factories**. A factory is where something is built. The factories gave many people a place to work.

21

factory   business where something is built

Making a Difference

President Roosevelt had to use a wheelchair. That meant he could not travel much. His wife, Eleanor, traveled for him. She became his "eyes and ears." Eleanor traveled a lot. She saw how people really lived. She saw the problems they faced.

Some people did not like it that Eleanor traveled so much. In the 1930s, most women stayed at home. They took care of children. Traveling around was left to men. But Eleanor was different. She showed that women could do many things.

Eleanor enjoyed her work. It allowed her to go places that most women never saw. For instance, coal mines were considered too dangerous for women. But Eleanor visited them. The information she gathered helped her husband. It allowed him to make better **laws** (rules). This made Eleanor Roosevelt a powerful woman.

Eleanor Roosevelt did many things that were unusual for women. Here, she visits a coal mine.

Eleanor Roosevelt

Frances Perkins

President Roosevelt helped women. His wife, Eleanor, was a strong person. She became an example for many women. The President also put many women in places of power.

Roosevelt named Frances Perkins Secretary of Labor. That meant Perkins set up rules. Those rules were for workers and companies. Perkins was the first woman to hold such a powerful job. Workers and companies often disagreed. Perkins usually sided with workers.

Frances Perkins was the first woman to become Secretary of Labor.

These auto workers are refusing to work until things get better for them. They are on strike.

Perkins also helped create **unions**. Unions were groups of workers. Unions tried to get higher pay for their workers. They also fought for safer ways to do work. Many unions went on **strike**. A strike happens when workers refuse to work until something is done to help them.

Under Perkins, unions gained more power. They were able to help workers. For instance, unions won shorter hours. Today, most people work eight hours a day. That started during the New Deal. Before, people often worked many more hours each day.

Marian Anderson

The **Great Depression** was very hard on black Americans. Most were poor before the Depression began. They had the hardest time getting jobs. They had a hard time because many white people did not like blacks. Many whites believed blacks were not as good as they were.

President Roosevelt helped blacks. He gave them jobs. Eleanor Roosevelt helped blacks as well. She helped them in 1939 by helping Marian Anderson. Anderson was a famous black singer. A group in Washington, D.C., refused to let Anderson sing. They would not let Anderson use their concert hall. She could not sing there because she was black.

This is Marian Anderson singing at the Lincoln Memorial. Eleanor Roosevelt helped her get this opportunity.

February 26, 1939.

My dear Mrs. ~~Robert:~~ Henry M. Robert: Jr.

I am afraid that I have never been a very useful member of the Daughters of the American Revolution, so I know it will make very little difference to you whether I resign, or whether I continue to be a member of your organization.

However, I am in complete disagreement with the attitude taken in refusing Constitution Hall to a great artist. You have set an example which seems to me unfortunate, and I feel obliged to send in to you my resignation. You had an opportunity to lead in an enlightened way and it seems to me that your organization has failed.

I realize that many people will not agree with me, but feeling as I do this seems to me the only proper procedure to follow.

Very sincerely yours,

Eleanor Roosevelt wrote this letter. She was angry at the group that would not let Marian Anderson sing.

Eleanor Roosevelt belonged to that same group. She quit and told people that she was unhappy with the group. Eleanor also helped Anderson find a place to sing. Anderson sang at the Lincoln Memorial. Many people came to hear Anderson sing. Both blacks and whites came. This was a big victory for black Americans.

End of the New Deal

The New Deal helped many people. It gave them jobs when they were poor. It gave them a place to live. New Deal programs made people feel good again.

During World War II, women were hired to do men's jobs. The men were away fighting the war.

Japan's attack on Pearl Harbor caused the United States to join World War II.

But the New Deal did not end the **Great Depression**. Hard times lasted until 1941. The Depression ended only after the start of World War II. The war began in 1939. The United States did not join the war until 1941. Americans joined only after the country of Japan attacked Pearl Harbor in Hawaii.

During the war, the U.S. spent a lot of money building weapons. This produced a lot of jobs. It created even more jobs than the New Deal. Factories needed workers again. People had money to spend once again.

Roosevelt remained **president** during the war. He died right before the war ended. People remembered him fondly. He helped people through two tough periods. He helped them through the Great Depression and World War II.

Glossary

agency part of the government

bread line place where free food was passed out

CCC Civilian Conservation Corps

civilian someone who is not in the army or navy

conservation saving or helping nature

corps group

dam giant wall that holds back water

Dust Bowl area in the middle U.S. where dust storms forced people to leave

factory business where something is built

FERA Federal Emergency Relief Administration.

Fireside chat radio speech by President Franklin D. Roosevelt

First Lady wife of the president of the United States

government group of people who run a country

Great Depression time in the 1930s when many people were out of work

Hooverville area where poor people built shacks during the Great Depression

law rule

mural large painting on a wall

NRA National Recovery Administration. This group set new rules for businesses to follow.

NYA National Youth Administration. This group gave jobs and job training to young people. It also gave them safe ways to spend their free time.

president leader of the United States

stock small amount of a company that a person can buy

stock market place to sell stocks

strike when workers refuse to do work until something is done to help them

TVA Tennessee Valley Authority. This group built dams that controlled flooding. The dams also created electric power.

union group of workers

WPA Works Progress Administration. The WPA was the biggest New Deal agency. It created jobs in many different fields.

Want to Know More?

Books to read

Freedman, Russell. *Children of the Great Depression*. Boston: Clarion Books, 2005.

Price, Sean. *The Dirty Thirties: Documenting the Dust Bowl*. Chicago: Raintree, 2007.

Ruth, Amy. *Growing Up in the Great Depression: 1929-1941*. Minneapolis: Lerner Publications, 2002.

Websites

http://www.pbs.org/wgbh/amex/rails/timeline/
Visit this PBS timeline to see major events of the Great Depression.

http://www.nps.gov/archive/elro/glossary/great-depression.htm
This website by the National Park Service has links to other helpful sites about the Depression.

Places to visit

These two historic homes are two miles away from each other. Both are museums that help explain the Great Depression and the New Deal.

Franklin D. Roosevelt National Historic Site
National Park Service • 4097 Albany Post Road • Hyde Park, New York 12538
General information (800) 337-8474 • http://www.nps.gov/hofr/

Eleanor Roosevelt National Historic Site
General information (800) 337-8474 or (845) 229-9115
http://www.nps.gov/elro/index.htm

Read ***Dirty Thirties: Documenting the Dust Bowl*** to learn about the dust storms that swept across the middle United States during the 1930s.

Index